Patrick

KNOWING RIGHT FROM WRONG

Thoughts from the Catechism of the Catholic Church

VERITAS

First published 1995 by
Veritas Publications
7-8 Lower Abbey Street
Dublin 1

ISBN 1 85390 294 2

Cover design by Bill Bolger
Printed in Ireland by Paceprint Ltd, Dublin

A man I knew was a witness in a court case in which it was being suggested that members of the defendant's family were sexually promiscuous. The witness agreed that the family was by no means a model one: the father had been in jail for sheep-stealing, the mother was a shop-lifter, a brother was a joy-rider, and two uncles were drunkards. But, said the witness, there was never any question of immorality.

There was a time, and not so long ago, when in the minds of many people the word immorality suggested mainly, if not only, sexual misconduct. An immoral woman was one who was free with her favours, not one who mistreated her children or failed to pay her bills. A man who lived off immoral earnings was one who exploited prostitution for his own gain, not one who paid bad wages or engaged in shady business deals. Immorality was sin against the sixth and ninth commandments, not the fourth or fifth or seventh or eighth or tenth.

Nowadays we seem to have broken out of this narrow view. We speak of the morality of tax evasion, for example, or of nuclear warfare, or of human genetic engineering. There is a demand for ethics in government and in the media and in the professions. We are aware of a responsibility towards the people we call marginalised – the poor, the homeless, those who are out of work. There is even talk of the rights of animals, and there is a growing awareness of the damage which we may be doing to the environment.

This enlargement of our understanding is good, for in truth morality has to do with all our relationships. Indeed, we could say that morality is about how we choose to relate with each other and with the world around us. For we come into being, and grow and live, in a complex web of relationships: with parents and family, with schoolmates and friends, with neighbours and co-workers – in short, with the community of which we are each a part. And, unlike other animals, we come to have some choice about the way in which we are going to relate.

The Power of Choice
I say we *come* to have some choice about the way in which we relate, because of course it is a power which we acquire as we grow older. At first our relationships are spontaneous and unreflecting: a baby doesn't decide how it's going to relate with its mother or father or older brother or sister, it just *is* in relationship with them as daughter or son or sibling. But as a child gets older it develops a mind of its own, and the time comes when it can choose to behave badly or well.

The power to choose is available to us because, as the philosophers put it, the human being is rational and free. 'Rational' here means having the power of reason, an ability to reflect and to plan, which includes remembering and imagining and considering alternative ways of acting. Freedom is the power of choice, 'the power, rooted in reason and will, to act or not to act, to do this or that, and so to perform deliberate actions on one's own responsibility', as the Catechism explains it (*1731*).

You could train a dog to behave in certain ways, but you couldn't get him to pick a present for your birthday. It's just not possible to train an animal to

4

choose in the way a human does. For the animal can't work out the pros and cons of different kinds of behaviour, and so can't really 'decide' to do one thing in preference to another. Some people have thought that human behaviour too is conditioned, in much the same way as any other animal's. But the balance of experience is in favour of a power in the human being to make choices, which is what is meant by free will. Otherwise we should have to abandon the language of praise and blame, merit and reproach, and there would be no point in trying to persuade.

Of course, like other animals, humans also have instincts – for survival, for example, or self-preservation. We also have needs and wants which move us to seek their satisfaction: a child cries when it is hungry or wants comforting, adolescence brings the onset of urges arising from sexuality. And we also have feelings, 'passions', as the Catechism calls them, 'emotions... that incline us to act or not to act in regard to something felt or imagined to be good or evil' (1763). The chief passions are love and hatred, desire and fear, joy, sadness and anger (1771).

Our instincts and our feelings are vital in the human make-up, but they are not the whole of it. For reason and freedom can allow us to integrate them in our personality in such a way that we are not at their mercy. That is what is meant by human growth, human maturity. It is the task of a lifetime, and we never quite get it finally right. But that is the challenge which human nature presents us with, the challenge of becoming more fully human, more fully ourselves.

Responsibility

Another way of putting all this is to say that human beings are responsible. This comes from a Latin word meaning to answer, and we can see how it fits if we think it through. We sometimes ask the question 'who is responsible?' – for the upkeep of the roads, say, or for a very fine building, or for the mess the country is in. At one level we are asking who *caused* something to be done (or not), or we might be asking who's 'in charge'. The idea is that whoever it is can be held accountable, answerable, and may be praised or blamed accordingly.

Reason and freedom are the basis of moral responsibility, for it is they which allow us to be 'in charge' of ourselves and our lives. They are the gifts which distinguish the human being and give us a special 'dignity', and we are answering to our dignity when we use them rightly and well. Not that we can always be blamed when we don't, for our understanding may be imperfect through no fault of our own, and our freedom may be diminished by forces outside our control.

That's what the Catechism has in mind when it says that '... responsibility for an action can be diminished... by ignorance, inadvertence, duress, fear, habit, inordinate attachments and other psychological and social factors' (*1735*). In other words, we can't be blamed for honest mistakes. Likewise, there's no use in preaching at an addict who is in the grip of drugs or drink, for the habit doesn't let him see straight, and it leaves him literally powerless. Someone who is paralysed by depression, or overwhelmed by a fearsome anxiety, is simply unable to obey the injunction to 'pull yourself together'.

For centuries there has been an awareness that responsibility may be affected by factors and conditions such as those listed in the Catechism. But nowadays we understand much more about the 'psychological and social factors' which it mentions. We know, for example, that judgement may be impaired or freedom affected by inner pressures of which we are not even aware. We know something, too, of the distorting effects of social environment, as when someone grows up in a setting where drug-use is the norm, or when the circumstances of people's lives are so comfortable that they never see a dole-queue.

So strong are the forces which mould our choices that it is tempting to think that we are not really free at all, and so to abdicate our responsibility. And undoubtedly there is a risk of the easy excuse: 'I come from a dysfunctional family', 'the drink gets the better of me', 'it's the system' – which might explain things, but again, might not. We have to take seriously the ways in which freedom may be limited, in ourselves and in others. But it would be untrue to experience, and dangerous, to deny the challenge of the freedom which we have. As the Catechism has it, 'this freedom characterizes properly human acts [and] is the basis of praise or blame, merit or reproach'(1732).

A summary may help at this point. The human person is distinguished from other animals by the twin gift of reason and freedom. And so we can make choices about how to relate to other people and to the world. It is in this that human dignity consists, and we answer to that dignity to the extent that we choose rightly and well. The Catechism puts it in a sentence: 'God created man a rational being, conferring on him the dignity of a person who can initiate and control his own actions' (*1730*).

Good and Evil, Right and Wrong
But rightly and well in terms of what? Why are some actions good, some evil, some right, others wrong? A religious person might reply that what is good is what is according to God's will, that right and wrong are laid down in the teaching of Christ and the Commandments. There is truth in this answer, and it would carry weight with someone whose sense of God is strong. But it needs to be probed, for it begs some questions and could be misleading.

It would be misleading if it gave the impression that the moral law is something like the law of the land. The law of the land is concerned with the ordering of life in society. The law in Ireland says that you must drive on the left-hand side of the road. It could be otherwise if the lawmakers so decided, as have the lawmakers in most other countries in Europe. Similarly with other pieces of legislation – about taxes, say, or schooling or medical care; they are law because the lawmakers said so, and we must obey them because they are the law.

But is this the way with the moral law? Is God like a lawmaker who, having made us, then decided to give us some rules to live by? Or is it that he made us in a certain way, and the rules follow from that? Are things 'good' or 'right' just because God has said so, and must we obey the moral law just because God said so, rather as we drive on the left because this is what the lawmakers happen to have laid down? Or is it the case that the Ten Commandments or the teaching of Jesus are a 'spelling out' rather than a 'laying down' of what is good and right: that there is right and wrong, good and bad, even if nothing were revealed or laid down?

This was the subject of a famous debate in the Middle Ages, which itself went back to Plato and other ancient Greeks. That should be enough to suggest that the answer isn't obvious. Yet most Christian thinkers have preferred the second alternative: that divine revelation spells out what is right and good and endorses it, and that what is right and good can be explained in terms of our nature as human beings. Put simply, their argument is that we couldn't know that God is good, or that his commands are for our good, unless we had an idea of what 'good' meant.

This is another way of saying that our reason can tell us what is good and what is bad. But good and bad in terms of what? We call a thing good when we admire it either in itself or when it is fit for the purpose for which it exists. So, for example, anyone could know whether a knife was good or bad, or a lawnmower, or a fire, or a book. But what about a good *person*? How would you recognise a good human being? One answer to this is that a good human being is someone who does good acts. But an act is good if it makes for the good of the person, so we are back to the question, what is the good of the person, what is a fit way for the human being to live?

The Point of Being Moral – Survival or Flourishing?

You could ask these questions from a different vantage-point in other terms. Take a few examples. We say that life is a good and that it is wrong to kill. Familiar moral rules include those that say that we ought to give people what is due to them, that we ought not to lie or cheat, that we ought to keep our promises. You could ask, what's the *point* of these rules and evaluations? What is it about the human being which calls for our behaviour to be shaped by them? An obvious answer is survival.

And, of course, this is true as far as it goes, for we wouldn't survive, as individuals or as a race, if people generally didn't honour these rules. Live and let live isn't a bad policy as regards our relationships with others; and it makes sense in terms of survival not to do to others what you wouldn't want them to do to you. But are we ever content with mere survival? Don't we want not only to live but to live 'well'? A better answer is that when we honour the rules of morality we flourish as human beings.

Again it was the Greek philosophers who shaped our way of thinking about this. Aristotle said that everything that exists has a point or purpose in existing. We will 'flourish' only when that purpose is fulfilled. Reason is the distinguishing mark of a human being, so we flourish when we act according to a rational purpose.

We are meant for happiness, the ultimate human good, and our achievement of happiness is how we flourish as human beings. Happiness comes when we live according to reason, according to our nature. You

10

could say that happiness is the ultimate human good, and that our choices are good to the extent that they contribute to our happiness. In fact we always choose according to our perception of what is good for us. But of course we might be mistaken, so it is necessary to try to ensure that we act according to *right* reason, and seek that which is truly for our good.

Later we'll see how this might be done, that is, how we can try to ensure that our choices are the right ones. For the moment the point to notice is that it is a key tenet of mainline Christian thinking that by using our reason we can sketch at least the general lines of how we ought to behave. This is the basis for the idea of a 'natural law', whose offspring is the modern notion of universal human rights.

One implication of this is that morality is not the preserve of those who accept the Christian revelation. This is an important point on several counts. For one thing it provides a basis for making common cause with people of other religious traditions or of none. This is what Pope John XXIII had in mind when he addressed his encyclical on peace not just to Catholics or even Christians, but to everyone 'of good will'. It is what has made John Paul II appeal so often to the right to life, and other rights which are nowadays acknowledged as belonging to our very humanity.

Peace and justice and all that is involved in human rights are the concern not just of Christians but of everyone in the world. We hear a lot about 'pluralism' of religious and moral belief and practice in today's world. Indeed there is much diversity, and it includes people who subscribe to none of the religions but who are as serious about morality as we are. But for all the differences in culture between races and peoples there is a common core of moral value. And the future of the global village may depend on how that core is ackowledged and built upon.

A second implication is that it is wrong to think of those who are not Christian as morally second-class. It's possible to be moral without belonging to a religion, and in the other religious traditions themselves there is much that can illuminate the moral search of the Christian. This is why Vatican II called for a 'dialogue', not just among Christians but with other faiths, and with secular experience also. A striking example of how Christians have learned from others is what we have learned from Gandhi about non-violent resistance. There is a special irony in the fact that he himself included Jesus among his mentors.

Living according to right reason may strike some people as a cold description of the moral life. The notion that we flourish in so far as we choose rationally, that human happiness lies in rational choice, could give the impression that good and bad and right and wrong are, as we would say, in the head. Important as it is to see that morality is a work of reason, it is also important to grasp that it is not just in the head but in the heart.

By that I mean that we are drawn to what is good not just because of its appeal to the mind. We do not perceive the value of life in the same way as we might perceive the corectness of an answer to a sum. For what is good engages our feelings, our passions, as the Catechism calls them, and through them it seeks to engage our will. It satisfies us, gives us 'happiness', because it appeals to our deepest desires. It is no wonder that human flourishing is so widely thought to lie in loving and being loved; and that in so many moral traditions the first principle of good behaviour is love.

Where Does Religious Faith Come In?

But if it is possible to have a morality without religion, where does religion come in? Perhaps the best way to approach this question is to consider the fact that how we behave towards other people depends on what we make of them, and what we make of others and of the world around us depends on how we look at life. An illustration may help to make the point.

The philosopher Thomas Hobbes said of human existence that it was 'solitary, poor, nasty, brutish and short'. Now, if that was your view of life, how would you be likely to behave? Someone who looks at life like that is bound to have negative and cynical attitudes. He or she must look on life as a battleground, an arena of perpetual struggle in which no holds are barred. Aggressiveness, competitiveness and ruthlessness will mark their dealings with other people. 'Nice guys finish last' might be the motto. There could be no place for generosity or mercy or fairness, or for any attitude or behaviour which wasn't defensive or promoting of self-interest.

Behind all our choices lies some view of life, some 'vision', even if we never articulate it fully, and even if we are unconscious of it. This view is expressed in certain beliefs about the way things are. It might be as crude as the belief that what can go wrong will go wrong, or, more optimistically, that whatever happens is for the best. It might or might not be so bleak and uncompromisingly negative as Hobbes', but it is what ultimately shapes the way we conduct our lives.

Many people's vision of life is provided by their religion, by the beliefs which their religion offers about humanity, its place in the world, and its destiny. The Christian's faith is that, in and above all the things of our experience, there is at work a provident, gracious God who has created us and loves us and wants us to share in his life. This credo shapes the moral life by drawing and empowering the Christian to live in faith, in hope and in love.

The Christian Vision of Life
And in doing this the faith of the Christian connects with questions which make themselves felt when we try to be moral. We might ask why we should be moral at all. The ancient philosophers answered this question in terms of human flourishing, of happiness. But is flourishing limited by our mortality, is happiness found only in gathering rosebuds which tomorrow will die? There is also the question of evil. Are our best efforts doomed because evil is, in the end, unconquerable? And there is the question of guilt, for our efforts to be good are always marred by our failures: are we trapped by the burden of our wrongdoing?

The Christian faith says that human flourishing is not defeated by death, that our ultimate happiness lies in the vision of God. The Catechism calls it 'beatitude'. This comes from the Latin *beatitudo,* the word which the medieval theologians used to translate the Greek word for happiness. What the theologians were saying is that the desire for happiness of which the philosophers wrote is fulfilled by the vision of God and a sharing in his life.

The Catechism expresses it thus: 'God put us in the world to know, to love, and to serve him, and so to come to paradise. Beatitude makes us "partakers of the divine nature" and of eternal life. With beatitude, man enters into the glory of Christ and into the joy of the Trinitarian life' (*1721*). 'Such beatitude surpasses the understanding and powers of man. It comes from an entirely free gift of God: whence it is called supernatural, as is the grace that disposes man to enter into the divine joy' (*1722*).

The New Testament, as the Catechism points out, uses several expressions to characterise the beatitude to which we are called: the coming of the Kingdom, the vision of God, entering into the joy of the Lord, entering into God's rest. The last three expressions refer to the completion of our happiness, to what is in in store for us, to what is yet to come. So indeed does the first. But the idea of the coming of the Kingdom is not solely about the future, for the core of the message of Jesus is that the kingdom of God is already begun.

The kingdom of God is the reign of God, the rule of God's grace in our hearts. The phrase has its background in the story of the expectations of the people of the Old Testament, linking in with their hope of deliverance through the coming of a saviour-king. The story is one of a gradual purifying of their hopes, a learning process in which their experience would disclose that the promised messiah was not a political leader but a spiritual one, that their deliverance was not to be from bondage to their enemies but from bondage to sin.

And so it is that Mark has Jesus, at the start of his ministry, proclaim the gospel in these terms: 'The time is fulfilled, and the kingdom of God has come near; repent and believe in the good news' (*1:16*). What Jesus is saying is God's reign is already here, already present in him. A riper theology would express this by saying that Jesus was the incarnation of God's love. The core idea is that the love of God, in all its height and depth, is revealed in the person of Jesus of Nazareth. And the call to faith is a call to faith in him, in his words and works, his suffering and death, and, above all, in his resurrection.

This is 'gospel', good news, the news for which the people of the Covenant had been waiting. It is good news because of the hope it offers in the face of the yearnings and the ambiguities of the experience of being human. It tells us that evil is not invincible, that where sin abounded grace did more abound, that we are not imprisoned in our failures, that there is a future for us and for our world.

'The kingdom of God has come near; repent and believe in the good news': the announcement of the reign of God is followed by a call to repent. Repentance in the Bible is a rich idea – not just regret, certainly not a paralysing guilt, but a turning round of our lives, a fresh start, a return to God. And the turning or return is possible because God loves us all the time.

Christian Faith and the Moral Life

What has this to do with morality? The Catechism points to one kind of answer: 'The beatitude we are promised confronts us with decisive moral choices. It invites us to purify our hearts of bad instincts and to seek the love of God above all else. It teaches that true happiness is not found in riches or well-being, in human fame or power, or in any human achievement - however beneficial it may be – such as science, technology and art, or indeed in any creature, but in God alone, the source of every good and of all love' (*1723*).

But love of God is expressed not just in prayer and worship, for the whole of the Bible makes it clear that you cannot love God unless you love your neighbour. The prophets denounced those who tried to please Yahweh by prayers and sacrifices while oppressing the powerless. Jesus taught that all the law and the prophets are summarised in the commandment to love God and the neighbour. A later New Testament writer was to say bluntly that whoever claims to love God but hates his brother or sister is a liar (1 Jn 4:20).

All love invites love, and the news that God is love is a call to us to love. We are invited to love him as he is in himself, but also as he is in creation, and especially in other human beings, for 'the divine image is present in every man. It shines forth in the communion of persons, in the likeness of the union of the divine persons among themselves' (*1702*). We shall return to this idea later, but for the moment, notice that the call to love is also a call to repentance. It has to be, for it is addressed to a humanity which is sinful.

Looked at from a religious, not just a moral point of view, sin is moral failure. Everyone, religious or not, experiences moral failure. We lie or cheat or take someone's character or break our word; or we let anger or hatred fester in us; or we wound someone by a cruel remark. We can be wrapped up in ourselves to such a degree that we are blind to others' needs, or so intent upon our own interests that we fail to give others their due. Not a day goes by without our compromising some principle, falling short of some ideal. St Paul's words are apt: 'I do not do the good I want, but the evil I do not want is what I do' (*Rom 7:19*).

Some of our failures we cannot help; as we saw already, not all that we do or fail to do is fully free. And we are hampered too by the sin that's in the world before us. We are tainted by what Paul calls the sin of the world, original sin, the brokenness which infects even the noblest human institution. Yet at least sometimes we have a choice, and we choose against what is good.

Moral failure is an impairment of our relationship with each other or with the world. But when viewed in a Christian perspective it is also an impairment of our relationship with God. For God is imaged in us and reflected in his creation. And if we do not love the neighbour whom we can see, how can we love the invisible God? (Jn 4:20) Our sins may be great or small: 'venial' – literally pardonable – daily failings which, granted the human condition, are almost inevitable; or 'mortal' in that, in their seriousness and in the degree to which we give ourselves over to them, they are enough to sever our relationship with God.

And so, according to the Christian vision, we are in need of 'salvation', deliverance from the prison of our sin. And in the Christian vision that salvation is available through Christ our Lord. 'Called to beatitude but wounded by sin, man stands in need of salvation from God. Divine help comes to him in Christ through the law that guides him and the grace that sustains him' (*1949*). The law, the moral law, stands in judgment over us and, being sinful, under the law we stand condemned. But the gospel tells us that we have not been left in our sin, that salvation awaits us in Jesus Christ.

The idea of salvation is one about which we have to be careful. People in Old Testament times made the mistake of identifying it with deliverance from their enemies, with political liberation. But it would also be a mistake to think of it only in terms of salvation of the 'soul'; for the human person is not just a soul *and* a body but a soul embodied, an embodied soul. The doctrine of the resurrection of the body is a corrective of a one-sidedly 'spiritual' idea of humanity. It is the *whole* person who is saved.

Another mistake is to think that salvation concerns the individual only. The Catechism puts this to rights: 'The vocation of humanity is to show forth the image of God and to be transformed into the image of the Father's only Son. This vocation takes a personal form since each of us is called to enter into the divine beatitude; it also concerns the human community as a whole' (*1877*). But if the community as such is called to beatitude, it follows that salvation has a community dimension.

Exploring this further we might return to an idea

already mentioned, that the image of God in us 'shines forth in the communion of persons, in the likeness of the union of the divine persons themselves' (*1702*). This idea recurs later: 'All men are called to the same end: God himself. There is a certain resemblance between the union of the divine persons and the fraternity that men are to establish among themselves in truth and love' (*1878*). The Catechism ties this is in with the fact that the human being is by nature social: 'The human person needs to live in society. Society is not for him an extraneous addition but a requirement of his nature. Through the exchange with others, mutual service and dialogue with his brethren, man develops his potential; he thus responds to his vocation' (*1879*).

Putting these two ideas together – that salvation is of the whole person, and that it has a community dimension – we can see that to live according to the gospel means blending action and contemplation in our lives. And we can see why the 1971 Synod on Justice could call working for justice a 'constitutive' part of the preaching of the gospel; for the transformation of human society is the formation of society in the image of God.

What has been said up to now is an elaboration of the point that the vision of life which Christian faith offers can illuminate our attempts to live rightly and well. It discloses the true dimensions of our flourishing, the happiness of the vision of God. It speaks to the experience of failure, in telling of a saving God who has not left us to perish in our sins. It speaks of grace, the free gift of God, revealed in Jesus Christ, and in the power of the Spirit at work in the world, sustaining and making all things whole. And so it offers hope, a hope for each of us personally but for the human community too – and indeed hope for all creation, 'that it will be set free from its bondage to decay and will obtain the freedom of the glory of the children of God' (*Rm 8:21*).

From this it can be seen that the way in which Christian faith enriches the moral life is not primarily by providing norms for behaviour, though of course it does that too. Its message is more fundamental, more far-reaching, for it tells us about what, by the grace of God, is in store for us and for the rest of creation. And in doing so it gives us hope, a hope that empowers us to take our part in the work begun in Christ, the work of building up the kingdom, as we await the time when God will be all in all.

'God created man a rational being, conferring on him the dignity of a person who can initiate and control his own actions. God willed that man should be "left in the hand of his own counsel", so that he might of his own accord seek his Creator and freely attain his full and blessed perfection by cleaving to him' (*1730*). We are back at our starting-point, human reason and freedom, the place where the religious and moral call are at one. The name which Christian thinking gives this place is conscience.

Conscience

'Deep within his conscience man discovers a law which he has not laid upon himself but which he must obey. Its voice, ever calling him to love and to do what is good and to avoid evil, sounds in his heart at the right moment... For man has in his heart a law inscribed by God... His conscience is man's most secret core and his sanctuary. There he is alone with God whose voice echoes in his depths' (*Gaudium et spes,* 16) (*1776*). So the Catechism begins its account of conscience, quoting a celebrated passage from Vatican II.

The Council and the Catechism here the conscience through the eyes of Christian faith, that is, as it is illuminated by revelation so as to show its true depth and breadth. But of course it is possible, as it is with morality itself, to give an account of conscience in secular terms – as it is, so to speak, at first sight. And just as it is important to be able to speak of morality in secular terms, so with conscience, as indeed the Catechism itself does, in line with the theological tradition.

'Moral conscience, present at the heart of the person, enjoins him at the appropriate moment to do good and to avoid evil. It also judges particular choices, approving those that are good and denouncing those that are evil' (*1777*). Here are summarised the essential elements: first, conscience is present 'at the heart of the person'; second, it 'enjoins' us to do good and avoid evil; and, third, it 'judges', approving and denouncing as appropriate.

We might start with the third element, conscience's judging function. The Catechism elaborates: 'Conscience is a judgment of reason whereby the human person recognises the moral quality of a concrete act that he is going to perform, is in the process of performing, or has already completed' (*1778*). Such a judgment is possible to the extent that the conscience is already, as it is said, 'informed': that is, in possession of relevant moral principles and in touch with the facts and circumstances to which the principles are to be applied.

But – the second element – conscience is said to 'enjoin' us, as it is also said to 'approve' or to 'denounce'. There is a suggestion here that while it is a judgement of reason it is not coldly rational, that our feelings come into the workings of conscience too. And indeed one could say that it somehow involves the core of the personality – the 'heart' is the metaphor used. Conscience belongs to the depths of our being.

Where does Conscience come From?

Are we born with a conscience? It seems better to say that we are born with the makings of one, for if conscience were innate we should have to say that a tiny baby knows right from wrong. What we're born with is a capacity for thinking and feeling which, when in due course it is 'educated', allows us to distinguish between good and evil, between right and wrong, and to make our choices accordingly.

Freud studied the way in which we acquire a conscience, and in the light of his findings we can understand the ways in which a mature conscience differs from an infantile one. The new-born baby is first and foremost a bundle of instincts and needs. It has an instinct for survival, of course, but it cannot survive unless its needs are met – unless it is fed, cuddled, sheltered, clothed. All its needs come down to a basic need, the need to be loved and cared for.

This love comes first from the parent – usually in the first place the mother – or some parent-figure. The child learns to identify love with the parent's approval or disapproval, and to 'organise' its various other needs in terms of the need for love. It learns, that is, that some kinds of behaviour provoke a smile, others a frown or a cross word. And gradually it takes in the do's and don'ts, remembering how kicking the cat made Daddy angry, imagining what will happen if Mammy finds it eating the jam.

None of this is thought out, for the child's power of thinking is still undeveloped. And by the same token the rules are black and white: share your sweets, don't hit your sister, leave the dog alone, stay away from the fire. There are likely to be more don'ts than do's, for the child's natural curiosity will ensure that it tries things out; and often its experiments have to be stopped, so that it won't harm itself or someone or something else. A small child can't absorb explanations or complexity; it's no wonder that the frequent response to its 'why?' is 'because I said so'.

So the process by which a child learns to behave is marked by three features. First, the rules come from outside itself, they originate in the will of the parent or parent-figure. Second, the rules are black and white, and they tend to be negative rather than positive. Third, and most importantly, the rules are obeyed on the say-so of the person who makes them, out of a need for approval or a fear of disapproval.

As the child matures is it gradually acquires the use of its reason, and in time will come to see the point of the rules. And some of them will in fact no longer hold, for their point was the guidance and protection of the child while it was still too young to think or fend for itself. They need no longer be black and white: staying away from the fire need no longer mean staying in the middle of the room, not going near the fridge can mean not eating all the ice-cream. As the child gets a mind of its own it can make the rules its own, doing things or not, not just on the say-so of the rule-maker but because it can see for itself what's right and wrong.

The Mature Conscience

Compared to the childish conscience, therefore, the mature conscience has three contrasting features. The first is that rules are no longer only in the will of an outside authority, but have been taken in and made a matter of personal conviction. Secondly, they are no longer simply black and white, for experience will have taught that there are grey areas, and a mature person will be able to handle the grey. And, third, a mature person will behave in a certain way, not just in order to get others' approval or for fear of losing it, but out of a will to do what is right.

Not every adult reaches this kind of maturity, of course, and in everyone there are likely to be traces of a childish response. Some people seem to need the assurance of a strong authority figure throughout their lives; for some, God or 'the Church' take the place of the parent-figure of childhood. Some will continue to prefer to live by black and white rules; grey areas make us uneasy, and some of us find them unbearable. And some will do what's right and avoid what's wrong merely out of fear of disapproval.

When referring earlier to the idea of morality as the law of God I indicated that the concept carries certain risks, and now we can see what they are. For it is possible to replace the parent-figure of childhood by God or by Church authority; to think of the Commandments as rules to be followed on the say-so of God or of Christ, without any need for reasons or explanation; and to keep them only out of fear, fear of the loss of heaven or fear of damnation in hell.

But if this is the way we live our lives we're not doing justice to religion or to morality or to ourselves. We're not doing justice to our religion, for the gospel is that God is love. We're not doing justice to morality, for we're missing its real point. And we do an injustice to ourselves and to the image of God in us, for our human dignity is in our God-given intelligence and freedom, the foundation of our capacity to 'do the truth in love'.

The Education of Conscience

A proper education of conscience is therefore vital to our religious and moral maturity. And such an education, summed up, is an education in understanding and in choice. Education in understanding means that we need to learn not just the Commandments, or what Jesus taught, or the precepts and teaching of the Church. We need also to learn the *basis* for the rules by which we live, the reasons why we ought to act in this way and not in that. Only then can we make them our own, only then shall we be acting from conviction, and so living up to our calling as rational beings in the image and likeness of God.

It makes sense to shape our lives according to the Commandments and other biblical teachings, and to the teaching of our tradition as mediated by the magisterium of the Church. For, as we saw, the Commandments are a revealed endorsement of what reason provides as touchstones of human flourishing, refined and fulfilled in the teaching of Jesus Christ. And in its magisterium the Church has a Spirit-assisted mode of guidance in the task of living the faith in today's world. But it would be wrong to treat these sources of illumination in a mindless way, without seeking to understand how they come to be what they are.

In that connection it's well to remember that in the moral life there are grey areas, that we needn't expect that our choices will always be black and white. Life can present us with dilemmas, with moments of choice in which there's good and bad, and it's not always clear what we should do. Aristotle warned against expecting the clarity of mathematics when we make ethical judgements, and St Thomas had a similar point when he said that in applying general principles to concrete situations, the closer you get to the concrete the less clear the answer becomes. This is because when making concrete judgements we have to take circumstances into account and, as the folk wisdom has it, circumstances alter cases.

The Catechism adverts to this: 'Man is sometimes confronted by situations that make moral judgements less assured and decision difficult. But he must always seriously seek what is right and good and discern the will of God expressed in divine law' (*1787*). So how are we to choose in such a case? 'To this purpose, man strives to interpret the data of experience and the signs of the times assisted by the virtue of prudence, by the advice of competent people, and by the help of the Holy Spirit and his gifts' (*1788*).

Of course there are some clear principles, and some rules which apply in every case (*1789*). It is not difficult to see that life, for example, is fundamental to human flourishing, and so respect for life is an obvious general principle. And it isn't hard to see that respect for life requires that as a rule we ought not to kill. But what if killing an aggressor is the only way to save someone's life? There isn't the same clarity about the answer to that as there is to the general principle.

Or, to take another example, it is easy to see why both confidentiality and truthfulness are important in human living; that is the basis for a general principle that we should keep confidences, and the principle that we should not lie. But it may happen that in a particular situation you can keep one of these rules only if you break the other; as when a woman asks a doctor if her partner who is his patient is HIV positive. Here again the answer isn't obvious – the application of a principle in the concrete hasn't the clarity of the principle itself.

This latter example brings up a point which is sometimes insufficiently appreciated: that changing times bring new moral problems, and old problems may be seen in a different light. Ours is the age of the Internet as well as of AIDS, of satellite TV and of test-tube babies. There are moral questions today which the race has never faced before. And old questions are posed in new terms. War is as old as humankind, and the ethics of warfare were a preoccupation of the ancients. But nuclear weapons are new, and the wisdom of the ancients says nothing about the morality of nuclear deterrence.

Some people are inclined to be impatient with debate and discussion of morality. Haven't we the Ten Commandments? they say, or the teaching of Christ, as though these ought to be enough to give us the answer to every problem. But this overlooks the fact that the Bible's teaching and the teaching of the rest of the tradition has to be applied afresh in every age, which means that each age must think things through afresh. One of the difficulties with our own age is that the pace of change is so fast that new problems are upon us before we have time to think.

So how do we ensure that our moral judgements will be the right ones? We try to inform ourselves as best we can, to make use of whatever help is available in the Christian tradition, to take advice when necessary, to be open to the voice of the Spirit of Christ. It is important, as the Catechism says, for every person 'to be sufficiently present to himself in order to hear and follow the voice of his conscience. This requirement of *interiority* is all the more necessary as life often distracts us from any reflection' (*1779*).

Virtue and the Moral Life

I've spoken of moral education so far in terms of developing an understanding of what the moral law requires; but there is another side to it also. All the knowledge in the world won't move us to act rightly unless we are disposed to do so. And we are disposed to do so if we are 'virtuous'. A virtue, the Catechism says, is 'an habitual and firm disposition to do the good. It allows the person not only to perform good acts, but to give the best of himself' (*1803*).

It's usual in Christian writing to distinguish between the 'human' and the 'theological' virtues. Human virtues, says the Catechism, are 'firm attitudes, stable dispositions, habitual perfections of intellect and will that govern our actions, order our passions and guide our conduct according to reason and faith. They make possible ease, self-mastery and joy in leading a morally good life. The virtuous is he who freely practises the good' (*1804*).

A sound moral education will therefore involve an inculcation of certain attitudes also – attitudes, for example, of conscientiousness, of fairness, of fidelity and perseverance. And this is a matter of practice, of doing the right thing so that it becomes a part of ourselves. As the Catechism observes, 'the moral virtues are acquired by human effort. They are the fruit and seed of morally good acts; they dispose all the powers of the human being for communion with divine love' (*1804*).

We need, you might say, to practise the virtues, for it is by practice that we acquire them. But the Catechism reminds us of an important truth: 'Human virtues acquired by education, by deliberate acts and by a perseverance ever-renewed in repeated efforts are purified and elevated by divine grace. With God's help they forge character and give facility in the practice of the good' (*1810*).

In the Christian way of looking at morality the human virtues are rooted in the theological virtues of faith, hope and charity; these are called theological because they 'relate directly to God' (1812). 'The theological virtues are the foundation of Christian moral activity; they animate it and give it its special character. They inform and give life to all the moral virtues. They are infused by God into the souls of the faithful to make them capable of acting as his children and of meriting eternal life. They are the pledge of the presence and action of the Holy Spirit in the faculties of the human being' (*1813*).

Afterword

Such is morality, in the Christian way of seeing life. It is a thoroughly human thing, a part of the experience of every human being. We cannot escape it, for we cannot escape the fact of our relationship with each other and with the world which is our habitat, and we cannot avoid the call of our human nature to choose how we shall live our lives. It is not something foreign to us, not an imposition, but rather the flowering of our humanity. The Christian's faith does not bypass the human reality; rather it discloses its fuller meaning, its true depth and breadth. In doing so it lights our path, in faith in love and in hope.